Authentic Ramen:

42 Easy and Authentic Japanese Ramen Recipes for Cooking Ramen at Home

CONTENTS

INTRODUCTION

Ramen has pretty much been a constant throughout my entire life. As a kid coming home from a long day at school all I wanted was a steaming bowl of my mom's ramen to hungrily slurp up. As a cash-strapped college student I remember those desperate hungover moments when I went straight to that hug in a bowl of broth, noodles, egg and meat to help me feel like a functional human being again. And as an adult my love affair with ramen hasn't lessened in the slightest. In fact, it's blossomed! The history of ramen is a deep, complex and varied one and my travels across Japan have opened my eyes to its endless possibilities. From a store cupboard student staple to a meal of delicate and complex techniques, ramen is ubiquitous. Although making a hearty bowl of this tasty soup can be time-consuming, it can also be quick as a flash. You can pour hours into making the perfect broth and noodles or simply jazz up your packet ramen with some tasty toppings and seasonings. Comforting, creamy, rich, spicy, sweet, sour, meaty, vegetarian, vegan. The possibilities are endless. And it needn't be an intimidating task. After all, Ramen is simply noodle soup. Simple in essence. Powerful in flavor.

In this book I'll be giving you a rundown of the history and cultural meaning of ramen, basic ramen building blocks and some regional variations that I discovered on my travels, as well as sharing with you all my favorite 42 recipes for home cooking. Some can be made as a quick meal and others require a longer preparation time. For simplicity's sake I've divided each chapter by the main flavor profile. Give one of these babies a try and enjoy a tantalizing trip to Japan within the comfort of your own kitchen. Although some may disagree on the absolute original authenticity and style of ramen, I have included recipes with authentic flavors and bases for your enjoyment and you'll find a few twists and curveballs here and there. Oh, and the bonus 'Weird and Wonderful Ramen Chapter' and yes, before you ask, the ramen burger does feature.

I wish you all well on your ramen adventure!

Happy Eating!

Aiko Takahashi

A Rapid Ride Through Ramen's History

So, when you think of ramen you probably automatically go to thinking that the dish is simply a Japanese invention. In fact, though, this is not so! The dish had its humble beginnings in China. Among other exports to Japan, the Chinese noodle appeared as early as 1488. However, noodles and broth didn't become popular until much later. Actually, it wasn't until around 1870 that people finally cottoned onto how good ramen was and began eating it everywhere!

Styles of ramen vary greatly. The basic principle of ramen is that it is made up of alkaline noodles and broth but, like a blank canvas, it can have any toppings added to it. Ramen in this form was widely accepted by the world because of the cheap ingredients that went into it—wheat flour, bones, vegetables and so on. This inexpensive meal actually fed troops in World War II and its popularity spread until restaurants started to serve ramen and dedicated chefs set out to become ramen masters.

There are many different regional ramen dishes and people still argue hotly about what makes ramen 'authentic' and about its origins and the political context surrounding these humble noodles. Ramen is a passionate subject for many people and there is even a museum dedicated to the noodle's history!

Nowadays home cooks and chefs alike are going further to push the boundaries of ramen. Ramen is no longer just a desperate processed alternative to turn to when you're poor at college! From the traditional steaming bowls topped with pork and egg and scallions with a rich broth to the radical ramen pizza, the humble noodle has never been so popular! It's a wonderfully versatile food and can be tampered with and changed in many ways. You may not be able to agree with everyone on what the best type of ramen is, but you should definitely be able to find a variation that you love!

Below I offer a brief overview of the essential ramen building blocks: the broth, the noodle and the toppings. I have also compiled a rundown of some regional classics that I have had the honor of tasting during my Japanese travels.

Ramen Building Blocks

It is important to remember that there are three main components that make a ramen: broth, noodles and toppings!

Ramen Broth Flavors

In ramen you have 3 main broth flavors—Shio, Shoyu and Miso. Ramen shops essentially use these 3 differently flavored broths to develop their own flavor profiles and try out new recipes and ideas. Depending on the chef or ramen master, extensive periods may be spent experimenting with ramen and developing secret recipes with flavorsome umami ingredients added to the broth. These ingredients can include animal bones, roast vegetables, spices, seaweed, seafood—the list goes on and on!

You may have heard of the popular ramen Tonkotsu and Tori Paitain. These, however, are not flavors of broth; they are both bases instead. Tonkotsu is a creamy pork bone broth, while Tori Paitan is a chicken broth. Both are heavily seasoned and are simmered for a very long time in order to get all the rich and flavorsome collagen from the bones.

Below is a rundown of the broth flavours:

Shio 塩ラーメン

Salty and lightly colored, shio ramen is nearly translucent and very light in terms of oil as it reduces to concentrate the flavor after boiling.

Shoyu 醤油ラーメン

Shoyu ramen can often be made up of a variety of secret ingredients added to the soy sauce. It can vary in color depending upon what is in it—it can be clear and brown and light to the taste or it can be heavy and dark.

Miso 味噌ラーメン

Umami-rich and heavy, miso ramen is the most complex of the three flavors. You can get miso paste as well as miso broth and there are many different variations.

Noodles

Ramen noodles go far beyond the dried product that you'll find in a lot of college kitchens! There's a plethora of different types of ramen noodles, and chefs will select different noodles based on different factors, such as their ability to cling and soak up the broth, their bounciness, their texture and thickness and how they complement the soup.

You can buy fresh noodles, dried noodles and you can even make your own—in the Chicken chapter I have included a recipe on how to make your own ramen noodles. There are many different types, but dried noodles bought like you would do pasta suit many ramen dishes.

You might have seen people eating ramen in restaurants and have noticed how they hungrily slurp up their bowlful and all its contents within 5 minutes flat. Many say that ramen noodles only last for 5 minutes before becoming too mushy and so patrons eat up their bowl as quickly as possible. That is typical ramen eating etiquette, so embrace tradition and slurp those noodles up!

Toppings

So, we've gone through the building blocks of broth and noodles in ramen, but what of the legendary toppings? Without toppings a bowl of ramen would be a lonesome soup bowl! They can range hugely, from roasted and boiled vegetables to juicy cuts of meat and fish to curried dressings, tofu and even chocolate! There is no dogmatic rule book on ramen. The upcoming recipes feature my favorite combinations but otherwise ramen is a blank canvas waiting for your creativity, so go wild!

Regional Ramen Dishes

There are many different types of ramen and the styles vary from region to region. Fortunately during my travels to Japan I was able to sample some of these wonderful dishes. Below is a collection of some of the classic recipes found in different regions and areas throughout Japan. I hope it inspires you to go and seek out some of these classics yourself!

Sapporo

Region: Hokkaido

Sapporo is a very well-known type of ramen. It's quite a heavy and rich ramen and these characteristics aren't by accident. Due to the freezing cold winters commonly found in Hokkaido, the chefs there designed the dish to fortify the residents. You can certainly imagine how the soup warmed them up, with the ramen's miso base, knob of butter, sweetcorn and juicy seafood. It's rich, unctuous and delicious.

Hakodate

Region: Hokkaido

This ramen also originates in Hokkaido, although it is rather different to Sapporo. While Sapporo is rich and hearty, Hakodate is lighter in texture and flavor. It begins with a clear shio or salt broth and to that broth there are added thin ramen noodles and fairly light toppings. The toppings often include thin pork slices and a sprinkle of spring onions. It may not look particularly decadent but you'll change your mind when you try this amazing broth. It looks weak and innocent, but in truth it is packed with flavor.

Asahikawa

Region: Hokkaido

Yet another delicious ramen dish hailing from Hokkaido! You can tell that I had a good time visiting this region and sampling the delicacies. Asahikawa is soy ramen. This ramen is also a wonderful winter-warmer and has a thin film of oil on the top, put there in order to keep the heat in the soup. So if you find yourself in the region of Hokkaido do make an effort to check out all three of these delicious soups if possible.

Kitakata

Region: Fukushima

Now onto Fukushima! Kitakata is very different to the hearty and rich ramen bowls. If you feeling feeble and want a light ramen bowl then this dish is deal. This ramen is a light and clear soy-based broth flavored with pork bones and dried sardines (or niboshi). The noodles also set this ramen apart as they are slightly curled.

Hakata

Region: Fukuoka

You may not have heard of Hakata but you may well have heard of the rich and hearty tonkotsu ramen! Tonkotsu ramen involves boiling pork bones for up to 8 hours until the broth looks a milky white and is suffused with deep pork flavor. Most people call it tonkotsu but this ramen dish is more accurately known as Hakata ramen. The ramen noodles served alongside it are quite thin and hard and are so in order to ensure that they don't dissolve into the soup too quickly.

Tokyo

Region: Tokyo

Tokyo ramen has wonderfully clean flavors of chicken and seafood. The dashi (broth made of seaweed and tuna flakes) is simmered alongside chicken stock and shoyu (soy sauce) and that gives the ramen its dark golden-brown color. This ramen is humble and flavorsome and represents Tokyo's beginnings as a city.

Tsukemen

Region: Tokyo

While some ramen dishes are classic and hail from decades ago, Tsukemen is a fairly new addition to the revered regional classics. This may be because it offers a revolutionary new way to eat ramen—separating the noodles and the soup. The soup itself is viscous and heavily seasoned. The idea of this ramen dish is to dip the cold ramen noodles into the thick soup/sauce mixture. Often, dashi is served alongside the thick soup and is added gradually so that the mixture may be drunk more easily at the end.

Chuka soba

Region: Wakayama

Wakayama ramen is also an ode to tonkotsu here. It features a thick tonkotsu-shoyu broth with thin noodles. When it was discovered by a popular Japanese TV show that featured the ramen, ramen enthusiasts started flocking to try it in Wakayama. Locals of that region, however, do not call it ramen; insteadr they call it 'chuka soba', which translates as 'Chinese noodles'.

Takayama

Region: Kyoto

Takayama ramen makes use of mainly bonito flakes, vegetables and chicken bones instead of flavored broths. Traditionally, ramen broth here is typically made by placing the base (known as kaeshi) in a bowl and dissolving it with hot soup. However, in the case of takayama, its kaeshi is boiled along with the base, resulting in a dark but clear shoyu broth. It also has a mild sweet flavor.

Onomichi

Region: Hiroshima

This ramen is arguably the most decadent and bolstering—mostly due to the fact that this is a ramen made with chunks of melted lard. The lard causes the ramen to come with a layer of hot oil, and the ramen noodles are known for being silky and flat. This is certainly a hearty winter-warmer. Certainly good to enjoy before a day in the snow.

Equipment and Kitchen Staples

Kitchen Equipment:

Large, medium and small-sized pots

Skillet

Deep fine-mesh strainer

Sharp knife

Kitchen scales

Ladles and measuring spoons

Spice grinder

Containers for your toppings, seasonings and liquids

Colander

Other recipes may call for additional pieces of equipment such as a pressure cooker or a Dutch oven. And, of course, if you want to go the whole hog and get the truly authentic ramen experience then by all means get yourself some ramen bowls, spoons and chopsticks for that slurpy pleasure!

Storecupboard Staples:

The upcoming recipes are my personal favorites for ramen, but if you have all, or some, or even just a few of these awesome storecupboard ingredients you'll be never far away from flavor at full impact!

Hondashi

Habanero powder (I buy them fresh, cut them, dry them and put them in a coffee grinder)

Crushed red peppers

Chili oil

Green onions

Leftover grilled meat

Carrots to make neat strips with (use a peeler and make long peels, then add to noodles just before done cooking)

Garlic

Toasted sesame seeds (bought fresh in bulk and oven-roasted)

Sesame oil

Ginger—fresh preferably, but powdered is okay.

Teriyaki sauce

Szechuan sauce

Sriracha

Lime juice

Lemongrass

Scallions

Cilantro

Crushed peanuts

Coconut milk

Soy bean sprouts

Red curry paste

Eggs

Spicy mustard

Rice wine vinegar

CHICKEN

Chicken is a wonderfully diverse ingredient and it's perfect to have in ramen. Below is a recipe to instruct you on how to make your own simple chicken broth, which will be called for in most of these recipes. You can use instant but homemade is always far superior!

Note: You can halve the time on a lot of these recipes by using rotisserie chicken or pre-cooked chicken instead of cooking your own chicken from scratch.

Classic Chicken Broth

 3-6 hours

Ingredients:

- 1 chicken (leave out the breast as an ingredient for future dishes)
- Salt and white pepper

Instructions:

1. Quarter the chicken by breaking it down.

2. Remove the breast from the bone for future cooking.

3. If you break the backbone from the chicken cage this will expose the bone marrow and add more flavor to your broth.

4. Put the chicken in a large pot and put on stove.

5. Pour in just enough water to cover the chicken and then one more cup.

6. Bring temperature up slowly to a medium to low heat and partially cover the lid. It shouldn't be boiling.

7. Leave to bubble for around 6 hours.

8. After 6 hours you'll see a lot of fat resting on the top, but don't worry—that's where a lot of the flavor is. Strain the broth with a straining cloth.

9. Voila! There you have an awesome-tasting chicken broth!

10. You can cook the chicken breast and use it for the upcoming recipes.

Warming Mushroom and Broccoli Ramen Bowl

This is a great and quickly prepared warming lunch or dinner to have any day of the week!

 2 bowls

 25 mins

Ingredients:

- 1 and 1/2 tbsps olive oil
- 4-oz pkt mushrooms, chopped
- 1 cup broccoli florets
- 1 clove garlic, chopped
- 1/8 cup fresh flat-leaf parsley, chopped
- Salt and pepper, to taste
- 2 cups chicken stock

- 1 cup shredded cooked chicken (consider pulled meat from a rotisserie chicken)

- 2 pkts Japanese ramen noodles

Instructions:

1. Heat up oil in an iron skillet on medium heat.

2. Pop in your broccoli, mushrooms, garlic, parsley and salt and pepper and fry for around 5 minutes or until the vegetables begin to soften and let out their moisture.

3. Add your tasty chicken stock and over a higher heat bring it to a boil.

4. Reduce and simmer for around 5 minutes over a medium–low heat.

5. Add your cooked chicken and ramen.

6. Simmer for 5–7 minutes more, or until the ramen is cooked.

7. Divide into bowls.

8. Serve hot and enjoy!

Sriracha Spiced Ramen Bowl

This spicy delight made with sriracha is made even tastier with the crunchy addition of peanuts and bell pepper.

 2 bowls

 15 mins

Ingredients:

- 1/2 tbsp olive oil or vegetable oil

- 1/2 red bell pepper, chopped

- 3 green onions, divided

- 1 clove garlic, chopped

- 2 cups water

- 1 and 3/4 cups chicken broth

- 1–2 tbsps sriracha (depending upon how spicy you want it)

- 3/4 tbsp rice vinegar

- 1/2 tbsp oyster sauce

- 1/2 tbsp soy sauce

- 2 pkts Japanese ramen noodles

- 1 and 1/2 cups shredded or diced cooked chicken breast or thighs

- 1/4 cup unsalted dry-roasted peanuts

- Sesame seeds (optional)

Instructions:

1. Heat up oil in a large pot over medium to high heat.

2. Add the bell pepper and 1 and 1/2 of the green onions and fry for 2 minutes.

3. Add garlic and fry for 1 minute more.

4. Add rice vinegar, oyster sauce, soy sauce, chicken broth, water and sriracha and bring to a boil.

5. When it comes to the boil add ramen noodles, cover pot and boil for 4 minutes.

6. Lower temperature and stir in cooked chicken.

7. Divide into bowls and sprinkle each with sesame seeds and peanuts and whatever onions you have left.

8. Enjoy!

Thai-style Ramen Soup

This tasty soup has a Thai twist to it which makes it lip-smackingly good!

 2 bowls

 35 mins

Ingredients:

- 1 tbsp peanut oil

- 1/2-pound chicken thighs or breast

- 1/2 tsp fresh grated ginger

- 1/2 clove garlic, chopped

- 1/2 sweet potato, chopped (skin removed if desired)

- 1 red pepper, thinly sliced

- 6 oz cremini mushrooms, sliced

- 1/8 cup Thai red curry paste

- 1/2 tsp smoked paprika

- 1/2 (14 oz) can coconut milk

- 2 cups chicken broth

- 1/8 cup soy sauce

- 1 tbsp fish sauce

- 1/4 cup creamy peanut butter

- 1/2 lime, juiced

- 1 tbsp brown sugar

- 2 pkts Japanese ramen noodles

- chopped peanuts, for serving

- chopped cilantro, for serving

Instructions:

1. Heat up a large pot over medium heat.

2. Add 1/2 tbsp peanut oil and the chicken pieces.

3. Brown the chicken for about 10 minutes or until cooked through and then remove.

4. To pot, add other 1/2 tbsp of peanut oil and then the sweet potato and peppers.

5. Cover pot and cook for around 10 minutes or until the sweet potato is soft.

6. Add mushrooms and cook for 5 more minutes.

7. Add curry paste and smoked paprika and stir until paste covers vegetables.

8. Heat up your 1/2 cup of chicken until piping hot. Gently mix in the peanut butter until smooth.

9. Place chicken back in pot and add coconut milk, remaining chicken broth, fish sauce, soy sauce, lime juice, brown sugar and smooth peanut butter mix.

10. Stir everything until peanut butter is fully mixed with soup.

11. Bring heat up to let soup boil.

12. Add in ramen noodles and cook everything for 3–4 minutes.

13. When ramen is cooked, divide soup into bowls and serve immediately whilst hot.

14. Garnish with chopped cilantro and peanuts and enjoy!

Superbly Simple Chicken Ramen

A simple and tasty chicken ramen with a jalapeño twist, if you should feel so inclined!

 2 bowls

 1 hour

Ingredients:

- 2 chicken breasts
- Salt and black pepper, to season
- 1 tbsp unsalted butter
- 2 tsp sesame or vegetable oil
- 2 tsp ginger, chopped
- 3 tsp garlic, chopped
- 3 tbsp soy sauce
- 2 tbsp mirin
- 4 cups chicken stock
- 1 oz dried shitake mushrooms (or 1/2 cup fresh)
- 1–2 tsp sea salt, to taste

- 2 large eggs

- 1/2 cup scallions, sliced

- 2 pkts Japanese ramen noodles

- optional: fresh jalapeño slices, for serving

Instructions:

For the chicken breasts:

1. Preheat oven to 707°F.

2. Season the chicken with salt and pepper and rub in.

3. Using a large and oven-safe iron skillet melt butter over medium-low heat.

4. Place chicken skin-side down into skillet and fry for about 5–7 minutes until golden and skin doesn't stick to pan.

5. Turn chicken over and cook for additional 4-5 minutes.

6. Place skillet in oven and roast for 15–20 minutes and ensure chicken is cooked through.

7. Take out of oven, place cooked chicken on plate and cover with foil for serving later.

For the ramen broth:

1. Heat oil in a large pot over medium heat.

2. Add garlic and ginger to cook until soft.

3. Add soy sauce and mirin, stir together and cook for 1 more minute.

4. Add stock, cover lid and bring pot to boil.

5. Take off lid and simmer for 5 minutes, uncovered.

6. Add dried mushrooms.

7. Simmer gently for 10 minutes.

8. Season with salt to taste.

9. Fill a large pot full of water and bring to a boil.

10. Add eggs and boil for 7 minutes.

11. Remove eggs carefully (but keep water boiling for noodles) and put into bowl of ice-cold water.

12. Let eggs cool and then peel.

13. Chop up your scallions and jalapeños (if you choose to use them).

14. Slice chicken pieces and set aside.

15. Add ramen noodles to the boiling water. Cook for 2–3 minutes until soft.

16. Divide the noodles into bowls.

17. Place in sliced chicken and the broth.

18. Garnish with scallions, soft-boiled egg sliced and jalapeños. Serve hot and enjoy!

Kimchi Ramen with Shiitake Mushrooms and Soft Egg

This ramen has a delicious Korean twist to it with the tangy and flavorsome addition of kimchi.

 2 bowls

 30 mins

Ingredients:

- 2 tbsp vegetable oil
- 4 oz shiitake mushrooms, stems removed and caps sliced
- Salt
- 1/2 medium yellow onion, finely chopped
- 1/2 (1-inch) piece fresh ginger, peeled and chopped
- 2 and 1/2 medium cloves garlic, chopped
- 3 cups chicken stock
- 1/2 packed cup kimchi, chopped, plus 3 tbsps kimchi liquid

- 1 tbsp miso

- 2 tbsps soy sauce

- 2 pkts Japanese ramen noodles

- 2 soft-boiled eggs, halved, for serving

- 1 scallion, thinly sliced

- Nori (Japanese seaweed sheets), for serving

- Watercress or other tender leafy greens, for serving

Instructions:

1. In a large iron skillet heat up 1 tbsp oil over medium heat.

2. Add shiitake mushrooms, season with salt and fry for around 4 minutes, stirring occasionally until mushrooms release water and begin to brown.

3. Transfer mushrooms to a plate.

4. Add remaining tbsp of oil to a large pot and put on medium heat.

5. Add onion, ginger and garlic.

6. Cook for about 5 minutes until onions soften.

7. Pour in stock and simmer.

8. Mix in the kimchi and its liquid, miso and soy sauce and continue simmering.

9. Cook ramen for 2–3 minutes.

10. Divide cooked ramen into two bowls and ladle kimchi broth over each.

11. Garnish bowls with egg halves, leftover shiitake mushrooms, nori, scallions and watercress.

12. Serve hot and enjoy!

Mexican Fiesta Ramen

This tasty and flavorful ramen has a taste of Mexico. The zesty addition of lime juice, smoky chipotle and creamy avocado really gives it an exotic twist!

 2 bowls

 30 mins

Ingredients:

- 1 tbsp oil

- 1/2 onion, chopped

- 2 garlic cloves, chopped

- 12 oz chicken breast chopped into cubes (or two cans chickpeas, drained)

- 1/2 tsp salt

- 1 tsp cumin

- 1 tsp chili powder

- 1/2 tsp coriander

- 1/2 tsp dried Mexican oregano (or a couple of bay leaves)

- 1/4 tsp chipotle powder or cayenne, or to taste

- 1/2 tomato, chopped

- 1/2 small can diced green chilis (optional)

- 2 cups chicken stock

- 2 cups water

- 2 pkts Japanese ramen noodles

- Juice of half a lime

- Avocado slices, fresh cilantro, scallions and lime, for garnish

Instructions:

1. In a large pot cook onions in 1/2 tbsp of oil over medium-high heat for 2 minutes, or until softened.

2. Add chicken and garlic. Cook for 5–6 minutes and stir often until chicken begins to look golden.

3. Add oregano and salt and spices and cook for 1 minute.

4. Add tomato, chilis, stock and water and increase heat to a boil.

5. Once pot is boiling add your noodles.

6. Turn down heat on pot to medium and gently simmer for 5 minutes, or until noodles are cooked.

7. Squeeze in lime and add salt and adjust to taste.

8. Divide into bowls and garnish with thinly sliced avocado, cilantro and scallions and serve with more lime if preferred.

9. Enjoy your Japanese/Mexican fusion!

Lemony Winter-Day Chicken Ramen

Lemon and chicken are two flavors that equal a match made in heaven. This simple soup marries the two flavors beautifully.

 2 bowls

 30 mins

Ingredients:

- 1/2 tbsp olive oil

- 1/2 leek, washed, chopped

- 1 celery stalk, chopped

- 24 oz boneless skinless chicken thighs

- 3 cups chicken stock

- Salt and pepper

- 1 pkt Japanese ramen noodles

- 1/8 cup fresh dill, chopped

- 4 lemon halves

Instructions:

1. Heat oil in large pot on medium heat.

2. Add leek and celery and cook for 4 minutes or until vegetables start to soften.

3. Add chicken thighs and stock and season with salt and pepper to taste.

4. Bring heat up to let pot boil, cover with lid and then bring heat down and let simmer gently.

5. Simmer for about 15 minutes or until the chicken is cooked.

6. Once chicken is cooked, remove it and place aside to cool.

7. Once chicken is cool, shred into pieces.

8. In the still-boiling water add ramen noodles. Cook for about 4 minutes or until noodles are cooked.

9. Remove pot from the heat and mix in the chicken and dill and squeeze lemon halves into the soup—add more to taste or adjust accordingly.

10. Divide into bowls and garnish with remaining lemon halves.

Soul Ramen

This is proper old-school ramen. You'll impress friends, family and yourself by making your special broth and noodles from scratch. There are a lot of steps and it takes some time, but when you're slurping this bowl of wholesome goodness I guarantee you'll feel one step closer to being an accomplished master of ramen!

 2 bowls

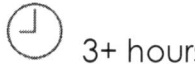 3+ hours

Ingredients:

For the broth:

- 1 carrot, cut into 1-inch lengths

- 2 scallions, trimmed and cut into 1-inch lengths

- 1/2-inch fresh ginger, peeled and thinly sliced

- 2 bone-in free-range chicken thighs (or 4 wings)

- 1/2 tsp sea salt

- 1 tbsp rapeseed or sesame oil

For the noodles:

- 1 tbsp sesame oil

- 1 cup flour

- 1 egg at room temperature

- 1 egg yolk at room temperature

  For the toppings:

- 2 eggs

- 1/2 small bunch chopped bitter greens such as bok choy or kale

- 1 and 1/2 tbsps finely chopped Japanese leeks or scallions

- 1/2 sheet nori, cut into four pieces

- Soy sauce, miso, or sea salt (to taste)

Instructions:

For the broth:

1. Preheat oven to 450°F.

2. In a large roasting pan put in scallions, ginger, carrots and chicken and season with salt and oil.

3. Roast in oven for 40 minutes.

4. Place vegetables, chicken and all juices from the pan into a large pot and cover with 8 cups of water.

5. Bring temperature up to the boil.

6. Lower the heat and simmer, keeping the pot covered, for 1 hour.

7. After 1 hour remove lid and take out just 1 chicken thigh. Place this aside in a bowl.

8. Cover thigh with broth, let it cool and then shred meat.

9. Let remaining broth simmer for 30–60 minutes more until it is reduced, probably to around 4 cups.

10. In a pot kept warm over a low heat, strain the broth and discard leftover vegetables and chicken thighs.

For the ramen noodles:

1. Combine 1 tbsp of sesame oil with flour with your fingers until you have crumbs.

2. Combine eggs and egg yolks and stir with hand until mixed in.

3. On a flat and clean surface knead the mix for 5 minutes until dough is pliable but not too gooey. You will have to knead it hard to work it into being pliable.

4. Let it rest for 10 minutes.

5. Using a pasta machine if you have one or a heavy rolling pin, roll out the dough to the thickness of about 1/8 inch.

6. Using your pasta machine or a sharp knife cut into linguine-sized noodles.

For the toppings:

1. Fill a large pot full of water and bring to boil.

2. Add eggs and boil for 7 minutes.

3. Remove eggs carefully and put into a bowl of ice-cold water.

4. Let eggs cool and then peel.

5. With the same boiling water cook bitter greens until tender.

6. Place in cold water with eggs.

7. Keep water boiling for noodles later—don't put them in yet.

8. When noodles and broth and toppings are ready, get out your bowls.

9. Add small amount of miso and soy sauce to each bowl.

10. Pour hot broth into each bowl and stir in.

11. Divide shredded chicken between bowls.

12. Put noodles in still-boiling water and cook for 2 minutes.

13. Remove noodles and divide between bowls.

14. Add more broth to each bowl depending on preference.

15. Cut eggs into halves and add to bowls along with cooked greens, nori pieces and the scallions.

Feel free to add extra seasoning as desired and be proud of yourself for your homemade bowl of soul ramen!

BEEF

Beef is a delicious source of protein and although it doesn't feature quite as much as chicken or pork in ramen recipes, it's still well worth including. From meatballs to grilled steak to hearty broths, there are endless possibilities!

Beef Meatball Ramen Soup

Meatballs aren't just for Italian dishes. This warming soup makes a wonderful meal of varied spices and delicious veggies.

 2 bowls

 30 mins

Ingredients:

For the meatballs:

- 4 oz lean ground beef

- 1/4 cup plain dry breadcrumbs

- White from 1 large egg

- 1/2 tbsp chopped fresh ginger

- 1/2 tbsp soy sauce

- 1 tsp chopped garlic

- 1/2 bag fresh broccoli florets and baby carrots

For the soup:

- 2 pkts Japanese ramen noodles

- 3 oz fresh sugar snap peas

- 1 tsp dark Oriental sesame oil

- Sliced scallions for garnish

Instructions:

1. To make your meatballs simply combine all the ingredients for them and mix together.

2. Get a little handful of the mix and rub together between your palms to make a ball about 1 inch thick, or bigger if you prefer, and place it on wax paper. Repeat until all the mix has been used.

3. Bring 5 cups of water to a gentle boil in a large pot.

4. Chop carrots in half diagonally and add to the boiling water.

5. Cover pot and cook for 4–5 minutes or until carrots are nearly tender.

6. Add meatballs gradually, one at a time, to pot and stir in.

7. Add meatballs to pot, 1 at a time.

8. Stir in the broccoli.

9. Reduce the heat, cover and simmer for 6–7 minutes until vegetables are tender.

10. Add ramen to soup.

11. Mix in sugar snap peas and boil gently for 2 minutes or until ramen is cooked and peas turn bright green.

12. Stir in sesame oil and divide soup into two bowls. Add further soy sauce to taste if you wish.

13. Garnish with scallions and enjoy hot!

Bell Pepper Beef Ramen

This bell pepper and beef ramen has a gutsy sauce that makes for a super tasty weeknight meal!

 2 bowls

 50 mins

Ingredients:

- 12 oz flank steak
- 1/8 cup cornstarch
- 1/8 cup vegetable oil
- 1 green bell pepper sliced into thin strips
- 2 pkts Japanese ramen noodles
- 1 and 1/2 green onions, chopped

  For the sauce:

- 1 tbsp sesame oil
- 1/2 cup soy sauce, low sodium
- 1/4 cup brown sugar

- 1 cup chicken broth

- 2 cloves garlic, chopped

- 1/8 tsp red pepper flakes

Instructions:

1. Slice steak against the grain into small, thin pieces.

2. Take a large-sized Ziploc bag and place beef and cornstarch in it.

3. Close bag and shake thoroughly until each beef piece is coated with the cornstarch.

4. Heat oil over medium heat in an iron skillet.

5. When the oil is hot add the beef and brown for around 5 minutes in 2 or 3 batches. Don't add all the beef at once because you want all the pieces to be browned evenly and not stick. Add more oil if necessary for subsequent batches.

6. Remove each beef batch and place aside on a plate.

7. Add bell pepper to skillet and fry for 2 minutes until it softens and then set aside on a plate.

8. Heat up a pot of boiling water for your ramen.

9. Keep the skillet on medium heat and add soy sauce, brown sugar, sesame oil, garlic, chicken broth and red pepper flakes.

10. Keep stirring and cook until you see the sauce begin to reduce and thicken. It should take around 10 minutes. Don't let it reduce too much as you won't have enough for your noodles.

11. Drop ramen noodles in the water and cook for 2–3 minutes until done.

12. Take the beef and bell pepper that you've put aside and put it back in the skillet and stir in with sauce.

13. When the ramen is cooked, add it to the skillet and mix everything well together.

14. Divide into two bowls, garnish with green onions and serve hot! Yum!

Crockpot Ramen Beef Curry

This is a mega-easy ramen–curry fusion that can be gently cooked over a long period of time. Perfect for making in the morning and coming home to at night!

 2 bowls

 10 hours

Ingredients:

- 24 oz boneless beef chuck roast cut into cubes

- 2 tbsps fish sauce

- 2 tbsps palm or brown sugar

- 2 tbsps red, panang or massaman curry paste

- 1 tbsp curry powder

- 1 tbsp ground turmeric

- 2 cups water

- 1 (14 oz) can unsweetened coconut milk

- 3 tbsps ground fresh chili paste (optional)

- 2 pkts Japanese ramen noodles

- Cilantro

- Scallions

- Lime wedges

Instructions:

1. Place beef, fish sauce, curry powder, turmeric, sugar, curry paste and water in crockpot and stir until combined.

2. Cook on low setting for 10 hours—maybe best to set an alarm or timer.

3. After the 10 hours, mix in the coconut milk and chili paste.

4. Boil a pot of water and add ramen noodles and cook for 2–3 minutes or until done.

5. Divide ramen noodles between bowls and pour over beef curry and combine.

6. Garnish with cilantro, scallions and lime wedges. Enjoy!

Sweet and Spicy Lager-marinated Grilled Steak Ramen

This tasty ramen includes two of my favourite things: meat and beer! It's a super tasty dish to share with friends and family and definitely hits the spot! Feel free to leave out the chili flakes if you don't like it that spicy though.

 2 bowls

Steak marinade 4–8 hours

Assembly time 20–25 mins

Ingredients:

- 1 cup lager
- 1 and 1/2 tbsps soy sauce
- 1/2 tbsp grated fresh ginger
- 1/4 cup canola oil

- 1 tbsp chili flakes

- 3 tbsps freshly squeezed lime juice

- 16 oz flank steak

- 2 pkts Japanese ramen noodles

- 3 scallions, thinly sliced

Instructions:

1. Place the lager, soy sauce, ginger, oil, chili flakes, lime juice and steak in a Ziploc bag.

2. Seal bag and shake to coat all ingredients.

3. Refrigerate for 4–8 hours and turn occasionally.

4. Remove steak from fridge and let it come back to room temperature on a plate. Keep the remaining marinade juice.

5. Get a small saucepan, pour in the marinade and bring it to a boil.

6. Cook until it reduces slightly and put aside.

7. Turn on the grill to a medium-high heat.

8. Season steak with salt and pepper and place on the grill.

9. Turn once and grill to your liking. Rare is 3–5 minutes per side for 1/2-inch thick steak. Medium rare is 5–8 minutes per side.

10. When cooked, take off heat and let rest for 5 minutes.

11. As the steak rests, boil a pan of water for your ramen and cook for 2–3 minutes.

12. Slice steak against the grain into thin slices.

13. Divide steak and noodles between bowls and top with a drizzle of marinade.

14. Garnish with scallions and enjoy!

Beef Ramen Noodle Soup

This classic beef ramen soup has an intensified and rich flavor from the chicken and beef stock and soy and sriracha. It's a perfect warmer on a long day!

 2 bowls

 30 mins

Ingredients:

- 2 tbsps olive oil

- 1 large onion, chopped

- 3 medium carrots, peeled and sliced

- 2 stalks celery, chopped

- 2 cloves garlic, chopped

- 1/4 cup fresh chopped parsley, divided

- 3 cups beef stock

- 2 cups chicken stock

- 2 cups water

- 5 tbsps soy sauce

- 1–2 tsps sriracha

- 2 pkts Japanese ramen noodles

- 4 green onions, chopped

- Sliced steak (recipe below)

- Onion powder

- Garlic powder

- Soft-boiled eggs

- Salt and pepper, to taste

Instructions:

1. Season thin-cut steaks with marinade of onion powder, garlic powder and salt and pepper (or you can use any seasonings you want).

2. Heat up olive oil in large pot over medium-high heat.

3. When oil is hot, add the celery, carrots and onions and cook for 10 minutes or until vegetables begin to soften.

4. Stir in garlic and parsley and cook for 1 minute.

5. Stir in chicken and beef stocks, water, soy sauce and sriracha.

6. Season with salt and pepper to your taste.

7. Turn heat up to bring soup to boil before turning down and simmering for 10–12 minutes.

8. In the meantime, take the seasoned steaks and sear in an iron skillet for 2 minutes on each side and then remove and slice thinly.

9. Stir the ramen noodles into the soup and cook for 3 minutes or until noodles are cooked.

10. Divide the soup into bowls and top with green onions, remaining parsley, slices of steak and a soft-boiled egg if you wish—see previous chapter on chicken for boiled egg method.

Homemade Shin Cup-style Spicy Korean Ramyun Beef Noodle Soup

This delicious recipe takes some time and calls for some unusual ingredients that you should be able to find at any Asian supermarket or online, but the result is a delicious medley of short ribs, kimchi and ramen!

 2 bowls

 At least 5 hours and up to overnight

Ingredients:

- 3-inch piece kombu (sea kelp, see note)

- 1 oz niboshi or shaved katsuobushi (see note)

- 6 scallions, sliced

- 1 tbsp canola oil

- 1 pound beef short ribs or oxtail

- 1 medium onion, split in half

- 1 (3-inch) knob ginger, cut into three slices

- 4 cloves garlic, divided

- 1 tbsp gochujang (see note), plus more to taste

- 1 tbsp doubanjiang (see note)

- 2 cups chicken stock

- 1 tbsp kochukaru, plus more to taste

- 1/2 (8 oz) jar cabbage kimchi, with its juices

- 1 tbsp soy sauce

- Kosher salt and freshly ground black pepper

- 4 ozs hon-shimeji or sliced shiitake mushrooms

- 2 pkts Japanese ramen noodles

- 4 soft-boiled eggs

Instructions:

1. Begin with covering the kombu with 4 cups of water in a large pot.

2. Bring to boil over a medium-high heat.

3. As soon as the pot begins boiling reduce the heat to a low setting and add the niboshi or katsuobushi.

4. Leave simmering for 15 minutes and then drain broth and discard solids before setting aside.

5. As broth simmers chop 3 scallions and set aside and finely slice the remaining scallions and refrigerate.

6. Heat 1 tbsp oil in a large pot over a high heat.

7. Add short ribs in batches and brown for about 10 minutes—remember to turn occasionally.

8. Remove each batch of short ribs when browned and put aside.

9. Add onion and ginger to the pot and brown—should take about 5 minutes.

10. Add 2 garlic cloves and the chopped scallions and stir for 3 minutes until browned.

11. Place short ribs back in pot and add gochujang and doubanjiang.

12. Stir everything until vegetables and beef are coated in spice mix.

13. Add strained kombu broth and chicken broth.

14. Bring pot to the boil and then reduce to simmer and cover lid, leaving a slight gap.

15. Cook for about 4 hours or until beef pulls away from bones.

    TIP: For best results, let it cool and transfer to fridge overnight.

16. After this is done, strain soup (if refrigerated overnight, you'll have to reheat it slightly until it goes back to liquid form).

17. Pour liquid into a medium pot and skim any excess fat.

18. Take out short ribs and transfer to a bowl.

19. Discard remaining solids.

20. When cooled, pick meat off bones and put aside and throw away bones.

21. Add kochukaru to the broth.

22. Put a fine mesh strainer over the pot and strain kimchi juice into broth.

23. Chop garlic and stir in.

24. Add soy sauce and season broth to taste with salt and pepper.

25. Bring to simmer to keep warm for the last step.

26. Heat remaining tbsp of oil in skillet over a medium heat.

27. Add mushrooms and fry until moisture is released and they brown.

28. Add chopped short rib to mushrooms and cook for 5 minutes whilst stirring occasionally until browned.

29. Boil a pot of water and cook ramen for 2–3 minutes.

30. Divide into two bowls and top with broth, followed by beef and mushrooms.

31. Garnish with sliced scallions, kimchi and soft-boiled egg if you wish.

32. Serve and bask in your culinary success!

PORK

Pork is very widely used throughout ramen dishes. You may have heard of the popular Tonkotsu ramen—a dish that is made by boiling pork bones down for a long period of time in order to get a rich and creamy broth, but you can incorporate pork into your ramen dishes in many other ways. Below are some of my favorite recipes for you to try your hand at!

Breakfast Bacon and Egg Ramen

This is a great ramen dish with two of my favorite breakfast items—bacon and eggs! If you want this ramen to have more of a kick then feel free to add more red pepper flakes and sriracha.

 2 bowls

 40 mins

Ingredients:

- 4 slices bacon, chopped

- 1 (1-inch) piece of fresh ginger, peeled and sliced

- 3 garlic cloves, sliced

- 1 tbsp chopped lemongrass

- Red pepper flakes, to taste

- 4 cups chicken broth

- 1 tbsp white miso paste

- 2 tbsps soy sauce

- 1/2 tbsp balsamic vinegar

- 1/2 tbsp rice wine vinegar

- 2 tsp toasted sesame oil

- 2 pkts Japanese ramen noodles

- 2 cups stemmed and chopped baby spinach leaves

- 1 shallot, very thinly sliced

- Soft-boiled or poached eggs (I usually do 1 egg per person)

- Chopped scallions

- Sriracha hot sauce

Instructions:

1. Place a pot over medium-high heat and cook bacon until crispy.

2. Remove and set aside bacon.

3. To the pot which still has the bacon residue inside, add the garlic, ginger and lemongrass and fry for 1 minute.

4. Add red pepper flakes, stock and simmer—remember to scrape bits up from bottom of pan.

5. Continue to simmer for 30 minutes and then strain and discard remnants of ginger, garlic and lemongrass.

6. Into pot stir miso paste, soy sauce, vinegars and sesame oil and keep warm.

7. In a pot of boiling water crack eggs to poach for 2–3 minutes or until white is firm, then take out.

8. Use leftover water to boil ramen noodles for 2–3 minutes. Drain and set aside.

9. In two bowls divide spinach, shallots and noodles.

10. Ladle the broth over the noodles and top bowls with crispy bacon, eggs, scallions and the dash of sriracha. Serve and enjoy!

Juicy Slow Cooker Pork Ramen

This slow cooker ramen takes some time but is utterly delicious. There may be some leftovers here but it'll keep perfectly well for the next day—if you manage to resist going back for seconds!

 2 bowls

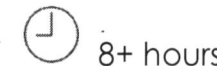 8+ hours

Ingredients:

- 3 lbs boneless pork shoulder, cut into 3 equal pieces

- Kosher salt

- 2 tbsps canola oil (if including the optional browning step)

- 1 yellow onion, coarsely chopped

- 6 garlic cloves, chopped

- 1 (2-inch) piece fresh ginger, peeled and chopped

- 8 cups low-sodium chicken broth

- 1 leek, halved lengthwise and coarsely chopped (white and green parts)

- 1/4 lb cremini or button mushrooms, brushed clean and coarsely chopped

- Low-sodium soy sauce, for seasoning

- Sesame and/or chili oil, for seasoning

- 2 pkts Japanese ramen noodles

- 2 large eggs (optional)

- About 4 green onions, finely chopped (white and pale green parts)

Instructions:

1. First of all, season the pork and rub it well with salt.

2. Heat up a little oil in a skillet over a medium-high heat and add the pork pieces in batches, browning them for 2–3 minutes, and then put them aside for later.

3. In the slow cooker combine pork, yellow onion, garlic, ginger, leek, mushrooms and broth.

4. Cover the cooker and cook on a low setting for about 8 hours. Check on the pork to make sure that it is very tender and fragrant.

5. When pork is done, transfer it to a cutting board.

6. Using 2 forks begin to tear away the flesh and cut it into small chunks. Discard any large pieces of fat as you do so.

7. Using a fine-mesh sieve, strain the broth into a bowl and discard any solids.

8. Skim off any fat from the broth surface.

9. Place pork and broth back into the slow cooker and season to taste with sesame oil, soy sauce, chili oil—it's down to your preference.

10. Cover the slow cooker and cook again on low setting for 30 minutes.

11. Fill a large pot full of boiling water and cook the ramen noodles for 2–3 minutes.

12. I often like to serve this ramen with a boiled egg. If you do too then pop the eggs into boiling water and simmer for 5–6 minutes, then remove them and let them cool so that you can peel them.

13. Divide noodles between bowls and ladle broth and pork over them.

14. Garnish with green onions and halved soft-boiled eggs and serve.

Sweet and Tender Pulled Pork Ramen

This super-juicy and delectable pulled pork ramen is best used with leftover meat from a pulled pork recipe or if you buy some pre-prepared.

 2 bowls

 20 mins

Ingredients:

- 10 to 12 ozs pulled pork shoulder

- 2 tbsps unsalted butter

- 12 ozs shiitake mushrooms

- 2 garlic cloves, chopped

- 4 cups chicken broth (though you can use vegetable or beef if you prefer)

- 2 tbsps soy sauce

- 1 tbsp hoisin sauce

- 2 blocks dried ramen noodles, seasoning packets removed

- 4 scallions, sliced

- 1 seedless cucumber, thinly sliced

- 2 tbsps chili garlic paste

- 2 tsps black sesame seeds

- 2 tsps toasted sesame oil

- 2 soft-boiled or poached eggs

Instructions:

1. In a large skillet add the butter and melt over medium heat.

2. Once the butter is melted add the garlic and mushrooms and stir to coat with butter.

3. Cook the mushrooms for about 5 minutes or until they are soft and set aside.

4. Meanwhile, in a large pot add the stock and bring to a simmer.

5. To the stock stir in the soy sauce and hoisin sauce.

6. If you want eggs with this dish then poach or soft boil and use the method used in previous recipes if you're not sure how.

7. In a pot, add boiling water and ramen noodles and cook for 2–3 minutes, then drain.

8. Divide cooked ramen between bowls and add the pulled pork, scallions and cucumber slices.

9. Pour the stock into the bowls and stir.

10. Add mushrooms to the bowls and more cucumber if you like.

11. Stir in the chili and garlic paste—it's up to you how much you want!

12. Add the halved eggs and nori sheets.

13. Sprinkle with sesame seeds and drizzle with sesame oil and serve!

Speedy Pork and Mushroom Ramen

This super-quick and delicious pork and mushroom ramen gives you big flavor in very little time! Great as a weekday meal.

 2 bowls

 25 mins

Ingredients:

- 1 oz dried mushrooms (preferably shiitake or porcini)

- Kosher salt

- 2 pkts Japanese ramen noodles

- 2 small heads baby bok choy, quartered lengthwise

- 1 tbsp toasted sesame oil, plus more

- 1 lb ground pork

- 1/2 tsp freshly ground black pepper

- 2 scallions, thinly sliced, divided

- 3 tbsps white or yellow miso paste

- 3 cups chicken broth

- 2 tbsps low-sodium soy sauce

- 2 tsps sriracha, plus more for serving

- 1 medium carrot

- 1 medium zucchini

- 1/4 cup coarsely chopped basil

Instructions:

1. In a medium bowl add mushrooms and cover with hot water and set aside.

2. Fill a pot with water and a dash of salt, bring to the boil and add ramen noodles and cook for 2–3 minutes.

3. During the last minute of cooking ramen add the bok choy.

4. When all is cooked drain the noodles and bok choy and rinse with water.

5. In the meantime, put 1 tbsp of oil in a large pot and heat it up over a high setting.

6. To that pot add the pork, salt and pepper and cook the meat whilst stirring, letting it slightly break up for 3 minutes.

7. Add half of the scallions and continue cooking and stirring until the pork is just about cooked through for 3 minutes.

8. Add the miso to the pot and stir and cook until it mixes together with the other ingredients for about 30 seconds.

9. Stir in the broth, soy sauce and the sriracha.

10. Drain the mushrooms that have been put to the side and add those to the pot.

11. Cover the pot and bring to a low boil.

12. After it comes to the boil, uncover the pot and reduce the heat to medium.

13. Simmer for 5 more minutes.

14. Taste the soup and adjust seasoning if you wish.

15. In the meantime, grate the carrot and zucchini using a grater until there are about 1 and 1/2 cups of each vegetable grated.

16. Now divide the ramen noodles, carrot, zucchini and bok choy between the bowls.

17. Top with the soup, basil, and scallions.

18. Garnish with sesame oil and some sriracha if you choose and enjoy hot!

Pork Belly Ramen

This delicious sweet and spicy pork belly ramen requires you to make your own broth and chili sauce—any leftovers are great for future dishes, and the homemade tare will have your friends and family raving for a repeat performance!

 2 bowls

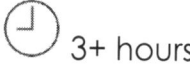 3+ hours

Ingredients:

For the broth:

- 4 chicken wings

- 1 lb piece of pork belly, rolled

- 2 cups good-quality chicken stock

- 2 tsps dried shiitake mushrooms

- 1 and 1/2 tbsps root ginger, thickly sliced but not peeled

- 4 scallions

- 1 tbsp kombu (seaweed)

For the eggs:

- 4 medium eggs

- 1 and 1/2 tsps caster sugar

- 6 tbsps Japanese soy sauce

For the chili sauce:

- 1 and 1/4 cups neutral oil

- 2 garlic cloves, finely chopped

- 1 spring onion, finely sliced

- 1 tbsp freshly grated ginger

- 4 tsps chili flakes

- 1 tsp sugar (optional)

- 1 tbsp sesame seeds

For the tare:

- 1 cup red miso

- 1 cup white miso

- 2 garlic cloves, crushed

- 1 and 1/2 tbsps sugar

- 1 tbsp mirin

- 1 tsp Japanese sesame paste (optional)

- 1 tbsp oil

- 2 pkts Japanese ramen noodles

- 3 and 1/2 ozs tinned sweetcorn

- 2 and 1/2 ozs tinned bamboo shoots

Instructions:

1. We'll start with the broth first. In a large pot place the pork belly and wings and all the other broth ingredients. Cover with 5 cups of cold water.

2. Bring heat up to have broth boiling before skimming it and turning down the heat again.

3. Put a lid on to slightly cover the broth and simmer gently for around 3 hours or until the pork belly is tender and remove the meat.

4. Whilst the pork belly is cooking prepare the marinated eggs, which also need time to steep. First of all, bring a small pan of water to the boil.

5. Pierce eggs at round end with a needle before lowering into boiling pan.

6. Turn down the heat and simmer the eggs for around 6 minutes.

7. Take out the eggs and run under cold water.

8. Whisk sugar into half a cup of water until dissolved and add soy sauce and stir in.

9. Add eggs into the mixture and marinade for 3 hours, stiring them occasionally.

10. For your homemade chili sauce put oil into a medium pot along with spring onions, garlic and ginger.

11. Cook on a medium heat until ingredients are golden.

12. Add chili flakes to mixture and then turn off heat completely.

13. Stir the mixture often until it is cool and then mix in sugar and sesame seeds.

14. Now for the tare. Mix all of the ingredients for it together except for the oil.

15. Fry the ingredients in a pot over medium heat for 5 minutes.

16. After all the items are prepared, i.e. the eggs and pork, slice the scallions and cut the marinated eggs in half.

17. Heat up the broth and then whisk the prepared tare into it.

18. Fill another pot with boiling water and cook the ramen noodles for 2–3 minutes.

19. When the broth is hot and steaming divide the noodles between the bowls and pour over broth.

20. On top place the egg halves, pork belly, scallions, sweetcorn, bamboo and a generous spoonful of chili oil.

21. Serve and eat immediately.

Classic Creamy Tonkotsu Ramen

Let's start with one of the ultimate ramen classics! This is certainly not a quick process and is time-consuming, but I guarantee it's worth it! Get ready to enjoy a creamy and rich ramen sensation!

 2 bowls

 8+ hours

Ingredients:

- 2 pkts Japanese ramen noodles

- 1 and 1/2 ozs pork fat

- For the broth:

- 2 lbs pig hocks and/or trotters cut into small pieces

- 1 lb chicken backs, cut into small pieces

- 1 large onion, peeled and slit around

- 1 whole garlic

- 2 inches ginger, sliced

- 1 leek, sliced

- 10 green onions, white parts only, cut in half across

- 5–8 slices of white oyster mushrooms

- For the pork belly (chashu):

- 1 and 1/2 lbs slab boneless pork belly, rolled and secured with string

- 1 cup water

- 1/2 cup soy sauce

- 1 cup white grape juice

- 1 tsp lemon juice

- 2 lbs sugar

- 5 green onions, halved

- 1 whole garlic, bruised

- 2 inches ginger, sliced

- 2 whole shallots, halved

- 1/2 tsp whole black peppercorns

- For the eggs:

- Sauce from chashu

- 2 eggs

For the seasonings choose one or a combination of any below:

- Chashu sauce

- Salt

- Soy sauce

- Tahini

- Miso paste

- Garlic and shallot oil

- Sesame oil

For the toppings and garnish:

- Enoki, blanched quickly in hot broth or hot water

- Black fungus mushroom, blanched in hot broth or hot water for a couple of minutes

- 10 green onions (green parts from broth), thinly sliced

- Nori (seaweed for sushi), squared 4 inches by 4 inches

- Garlic, sliced and fried until crispy

Instructions:

For the broth:

1. Place the pork bones, marrow and chicken in a large pot.

2. Cover all the meat and bones fully with water.

3. Cover pot with lid and over a high heat bring the water to a boil.

4. Once the water is boiling drain the bones.

5. Scrub off any dark marrow or leftover blood from the pork with cold water—this determines the color of the broth. If you leave these things on the pork then the broth will be brown as opposed to cream-colored.

6. Rinse out the pot and place the bones back in and then add the rest of the broth ingredients.

7. Add enough water to just barely cover all ingredients and cover with lid.

8. Bring the water to a boil over a high heat.

9. Once it has boiled, uncover the pot and remove and wipe away any scum that might have accumulated over the first 15–20 minutes.

10. Reduce heat to allow pot to simmer on low for 6–12 hours on the stove. (If you have a slow cooker then make this time 12–18 hours).

11. Check the pot after the first 10–15 minutes, after checking heat to ensure that it is barely simmering.

12. 2 hours before it is completely done, strain the pork fat and add to broth.

13. Cover the pot and allow the fat to cook until it is soft and tender.

14. Drain and finely mince pork before setting aside.

15. It is up to you whether you want to skim some or all or none of the fat from the broth. It depends how much

you'd like, but more fat adds more of a creamy flavour.

For the pork belly (chashu):

1. Preheat the oven to 250°F.

2. Place the pork belly in a pot and add water to fully cover it.

3. Turn up heat to get water to boil.

4. Once the water has boiled then drain and remove the scum that has accumulated.

5. In that same pot place the pork back inside and add the remaining ingredients listed for the chashu.

6. When the ingredients are added cover the pot with a lid and over a higher heat bring the sauce to a boil.

7. Once it has boiled transfer the pot to the preheated oven.

8. Cook for 5 hours.

9. After 2 hours of the pork cooking, take the pot out and shake it to ensure sauce covers the pork.

10. Afterwards shake once every hour until the 5 hours are up.

11. Test the pork belly by inserting a skewer inside. If it slips in and feels soft then it's ready but cook it for longer if you want the meat even softer.

12. After the pork belly is cooked to your liking, allow it to cool and then place in fridge.

13. Now prepare the eggs below to be refrigerated alongside the pork belly for a long period of time.

For the eggs:

1. Select a medium-sized pot and cover with water sufficient to cover eggs when boiling, then turn up temperature to medium-high to bring to a boil.

2. Once water is boiling lift eggs gently into the water and let simmer for 6 minutes.

3. Drain water and peel eggs after they have cooled.

4. Once you have peeled the eggs, place them into the cooled chashu sauce.

5. Soak a paper towel with the chashu sauce and place over eggs to ensure the tops of them are marinated too.

6. Marinate these for 4–12 hours in the fridge, alongside the pork belly.

Assembling:

1. Bring your broth to the boil and season to taste.

2. In a pot add boiling water and the noodles to cook for 2–3 minutes.

3. Cook noodles and then drain.

4. Divide ramen noodles into bowls.

5. Take the pork out of the fridge and slice.

6. Take out marinated eggs and carefully slice in half.

7. Place the broth in bowls of noodles and then arrange with the chashu, egg and some minced pork fat. Garnish with above toppings of choice.

8. Serve hot immediately!

Note: Season your Tonkotsu however you like—you can use soy, sesame oil, garlic, chili etc. Go mad!

SEAFOOD

Adding seafood such as shrimp, salmon and even lobster to ramen is a great way to spruce it up.

Super-easy Shrimp Ramen

This quick and tasty shrimp ramen is super-easy to put together and has a delicious Thai twist with the coconut milk and lime.

 2 bowls

 10 mins

Ingredients:

- 1 can lite coconut milk

- 2 cups shredded carrots

- 1 medium onion

- 12 oz raw medium shrimp

- 2 pkts Japanese ramen noodles

- 1 tbsp fish sauce

- 4 ozs snow peas

- 1/4 cup finely chopped cilantro

- 4 tsps fresh lime juice

Instructions:

1. Put 2 and 1/4 cups of water, the coconut milk, carrots and onion Into a large pot and bring it up to medium-high heat to boil.

2. Prepare snow peas by grasping the stem end and pulling to remove the string.

3. Add shrimp, ramen noodles and snow peas and mix all together.

4. Bring down heat to simmer for 2–3 minutes until shrimp is cooked.

5. Remove pot from heat and add fish sauce, cilantro, lime juice and salt to taste.

6. Serve hot and enjoy!

Creamy Peanut and Coconut Shrimp Ramen

Extra chili and peanut butter make this shrimp ramen a creamy delight!

 2 bowls

 15 mins

Ingredients:

- 2 pkts Japanese ramen noodles

- 1/2 cup coconut milk

- 1/3 cup creamy peanut butter

- 2 tbsps fresh lime juice

- 1/4 tsp red pepper flakes (optional)

- 1 lb cooked, cleaned, peeled and deveined large shrimp

- Half a seedless cucumber

- 4 scallions

- Lime wedges, for serving

Instructions:

1. In a large pot bring 4 cups of water to the boil and add ramen noodles.

2. Cook ramen for 2–3 minutes.

3. Meanwhile, in a large bowl, mix together the coconut milk, peanut butter, red pepper and lime juice.

4. Drain noodles and pour into the bowl with dressing and add shrimp, cucumber and scallions.

5. Toss all together until well mixed and divide between two bowls.

6. Garnish with lime wedges for squeezing and enjoy!

Sriracha Shrimp Ramen Bowl

Spicy sriracha and shrimp is a wonderfully warming combination, making this meal a tasty treat any night of the week!

 2 bowls

 20 mins

Ingredients:

- 1 and 1/2 tbsps sesame oil

- 1/4 pound large shrimp, peeled

- 1 tsp dried basil

- 1/2 tsp salt

- 1/2 tsp black pepper

- 2 tbsps sriracha hot sauce

- 1 small yellow onion, chopped

- 1 small red bell pepper, chopped

- 1 tbsp ginger, grated

- 3 cloves garlic, chopped
- 2 cups chicken stock
- 2 cups water
- 2 tbsps tomato paste
- 1/2 tsp garlic powder
- 1/2 tsp onion powder
- 1/2 tsp celery salt
- 1 and 1/2 tbsps soy sauce
- 1 tsp rice vinegar
- 2 pkts Japanese ramen noodles
- 1 cup baby spinach, roughly chopped
- 2 tbsps fresh lemon juice

Instructions:

1. In a large pot, heat 1 tbsp sesame oil over medium-high heat.

2. When oil is hot add shrimp and season with basil, salt and pepper.

3. Cook shrimp for 1 minute each side or until pink and firm.

4. Take out shrimp and place on chopping board.

5. In the same pot add remaining sesame oil and reduce heat to a medium setting.

6. Put in sriracha, red bell pepper and yellow onion and fry for 4 minutes or until onion and pepper soften slightly.

7. Add garlic and ginger and cook for 1 more minute, stirring occasionally.

8. Add water and chicken broth to soup pot and stir well.

9. Turn heat up to get soup to a boil.

10. Add tomato paste, onion and garlic powder, soy sauce, rice vinegar and celery salt and stir.

11. Reduce heat again to medium and simmer for 8 minutes.

12. Cut cooked shrimp into small pieces and chop spinach. Set both aside.

13. Add ramen to broth and cook for 2–3 minutes.

14. Stir cooked shrimp, lemon juice and spinach into broth and mix.

15. Remove from heat and taste soup—adjust flavoring if necessary.

16. Divide soup into two bowls and serve hot!

Super Salmon and Veggie Ramen

This virtuous and healthy salmon and vegetable ramen is a great protein-rich meal with delicate flavors.

 2 bowls

 30 mins

Ingredients:

- 4 cups water

- 4 cups broccoli florets

- 1 large carrot

- 1 large celery stalk

- 2 pkts Japanese ramen noodles

- 2 cups chicken stock

- 2 pieces salmon fillet

- 6 ozs snow peas

- 1 tbsp fish sauce

- 1 tsp Asian sesame oil

- 1/4 tsp salt

- Sprig of dill.

Instructions:

1. Preheat oven to 750°F.

2. Pour water into a large pot and then broccoli, celery, carrot, chicken stock and fish sauce.

3. Turn up heat until soup is boiling.

4. In the meantime, line a baking pan and place salmon fillets inside.

5. Season salmon with salt and pepper and put in oven to cook for 12–15 minutes or until salmon is opaque. Turn halfway through cooking.

6. To the boiling soup, add snow peas and ramen.

7. Cook for 2–3 minutes and remove from heat.

8. Stir in sesame oil, salt and juices from cooked salmon.

9. Divide soup between two bowls and top with piece of cooked salmon and garnish with sprig of dill. Enjoy!

Luxurious Lobster Ramen

This decadent and delicious lobster ramen is perfect for a special occasion. You'll have to make your own or buy lobster stock, but that's where the deep flavor of the dish comes from.

 2 bowls

 25 mins

Ingredients:

- 2 cups white wine

- 1 shallot, thinly sliced

- 12 peppercorns

- 1/2 cup white wine vinegar

- 1/2 cup heavy cream

- 1 pound unsalted butter

- 4 cups lobster stock

- 4 tbsps miso

- 1/2 tsp white pepper

- 2 tbsps lemon juice

- Sea salt, as needed

- 2 pkts Japanese ramen noodles

- 1 cup edamame beans, shelled

- 1 and 1/4 pound lobster, cooked, meat removed

- 3 scallions sliced

Instructions:

1. Pour the white wine into a large pot and add shallots, peppercorns and white wine vinegar, then reduce over a medium heat until 2 tbsps remain. Should take around 10 minutes.

2. Pour in heavy cream and spend 2–3 minutes reducing mixture by half the amount on heat.

3. Add 3/4 pound of butter and stir to make a beurre blanc.

4. Strain mixture and keep warm.

5. In another pan, pour lobster stock and bring heat up to let it simmer.

6. Add 2 tbsps of miso and season to taste with pepper and salt and lemon juice.

7. In another pan, fill with water and cook ramen noodles for 2–3 minutes and drain.

8. In an iron skillet, melt the remaining butter and stir in leftover miso and add edamame beans.

9. Cut lobster meat into several pieces and add to skillet and coat with sauce.

10. Stir in cooked noodles with 1 cup of beurre blanc sauce and season with salt and pepper. Divide between two bowls and top with the lobster and scallions.

11. On top pour the miso lobster broth into each bowl.

12. Enjoy your luxurious ramen feast!

VEGETARIAN & VEGAN

These delicious vegetarian and vegan recipes go down a storm and will appeal to meat lovers as well!

Vegan Vietnamese-style Peanut Ramen Salad

This super-easy and quick salad is a great way to use ramen! Make it for a quick meal any day of the week.

 2 bowls

 15 mins

Ingredients:

- 2 pkts Japanese ramen noodles

- 1/2 cup peanut butter

- 1/4 cup water

- 1/4 cup vinegar

- 1/4 cup teriyaki sauce

- 1/4 tsp chopped garlic

- 1/4 tsp crushed red pepper flakes (optional)

- 1 cucumber, quartered lengthwise

- 2 carrots

- 2 scallions

Instructions:

1. In a medium-sized pot bring 4 cups of water to the boil on medium heat.

2. Add ramen noodles and boil for 2–3 minutes or until cooked.

3. Drain and rinse under cold water.

4. In another bowl whisk the peanut butter, water, garlic, teriyaki sauce, vinegar and crushed red pepper until mixture is smooth.

5. Stir in noodles, cucumber, carrots and scallions.

6. Toss all together until thoroughly mixed and serve!

Sriracha Delight Ramen Soup Bowl

Super-quick, tangy, spicy and delicious: the sriracha adds a wonderful kick to this dish! Note: you will need a food processor for this recipe.

 2 bowls

 20 mins

Ingredients:

- 2 tbsps sesame oil

- 2 tbsps sriracha hot sauce

- 1 small onion, chopped

- 1 small tomato, chopped

- 1 tbsp ginger, grated

- 3 cloves garlic, chopped

- 1/2 tsp garlic powder

- 1/2 tsp celery salt

- 2 cups water

- 4 cups vegetable broth

- 1 tbsp soy sauce

- 1 tsp rice vinegar

- 2 pkts Japanese ramen noodles

- 1/2 cup scallions, chopped

- 1/2 cup cilantro, chopped

- 2 poached eggs (optional)

Instructions:

1. In a large pot put in the sesame oil and sriracha and simmer over a medium heat.

2. Add tomato and onion and cook for 4 minutes, whilst stirring now and then.

3. Add ginger, seasonings and garlic and continue cooking for 2 minutes.

4. Pour in 2 cups of water and then transfer whole mixture to a food processor or blender and blend until smooth.

5. Pour the blended mixture back into the pot and add the broth.

6. Reduce heat to a simmer and place in soy sauce and vinegar and continue to simmer gently for 8–10 minutes.

7. Taste and adjust salt and pepper and seasonings if necessary.

8. Add the ramen to the broth and cook for 2–3 minutes or until noodles are done.

9. Ladle soup into bowls and top with scallions, cilantro and the eggs (if you like) and enjoy!

Colorful Chili and Honey Tofu Ramen

This tofu ramen is colorful and gutsy with the mix of honey, turmeric, chili and soy. Certainly packs a punch!

 2 bowls

 20 mins

Ingredients:

- 1 tbsp olive oil

- 5 radishes, thinly sliced

- 1 tbsp rice wine vinegar

- A squeeze of honey or maple syrup

- 2 pkts Japanese ramen noodles

- 1/4 cup kale

- 1 tbsp soy sauce

- 1/2 cup firm tofu

- 1 pint unsweetened almond milk

- 1 and 1/2 tbsps chili miso (recipe below)

- A pinch of turmeric

Instructions:

1. Place the sliced radishes in a small bowl along with the rice wine vinegar and a squeeze of honey (or maple syrup) depending on taste. Mix well together and put aside.

2. Bring a pot of water to the boil and add the ramen noodles and cook for 2–3 minutes and then drain.

3. Whilst ramen is cooking, mix the kale with the soy sauce and divide between 2 bowls.

4. Heat an iron skillet with the olive oil over a medium heat.

5. Cut the tofu into small chunks and add to the skillet and fry for 5–7 minutes or until golden brown. Set aside.

6. Cut the tofu into pieces and divide between the bowls.

7. In a small pan heat up the almond milk until just hot.

8. Place chili miso and turmeric in another little bowl and add a small amount of hot almond milk.

9. Mix altogether to thin the mixture out and then pour into pan of milk.

10. Place cooked noodles in the two bowls and pour over broth.

11. Enjoy!

Vegan Roast Veggie, Garlic and Miso Ramen Bowl

This warming and comforting roasted vegetable ramen bowl has the tasty tang of miso and garlic to bring it up a notch. This recipe takes longer as you'll be making your own broth and there are a fair few steps, but believe me, the results are worth it!

 2 bowls

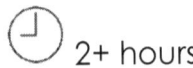 2+ hours

Ingredients:

- 3 tbsps canola oil

- 1 yellow onion, coarsely chopped

- 1 large leek, trimmed and roughly chopped

- 4 cloves garlic, chopped

- 1 (2-inch) piece fresh ginger, peeled and chopped

- 1 oz dried shiitake mushrooms

- 2 sweet potatoes (about 1 pound), peeled and cut into small cubes

- 1 head of garlic

- 1 pound fresh shiitake mushrooms, brushed clean and sliced

- Low-sodium soy sauce or tamari, for seasoning

- 2 pkts Japanese ramen noodles

- 1/4 cup white or yellow miso

- 4 green onions, chopped

Instructions:

1. In a large pot, heat 2 tbsps of oil over a medium-high heat.

2. Add yellow onion and season with salt then brown for about 5 minutes.

3. Add garlic, leek, ginger and dried mushrooms and 6 cups of water.

4. Stir all together and scrape up any bits from the bottom of the pot.

5. Reduce heat to medium-low and cover the pot partially with a lid.

6. Simmer for about 1 hour.

7. Strain broth through the strainer and get rid of solids.

8. Preheat oven to 400°F.

9. To a baking sheet add sweet potatoes and drizzle with oil and mix together until potatoes are mostly coated.

10. Cut off the head of the garlic and throw the rest away.

11. Drizzle garlic head with a bit of oil and wrap it in oil, then add it to the pan along with sweet potatoes.

12. Roast for about 45 minutes or until potatoes are slightly brown. Stir all vegetables occasionally too and then take out of oven.

13. In a blender or food processor add the roasted garlic cloves, 1/3 cup of the cooked sweet potatoes and 1/2 cup of broth.

14. Blend everything together and then add to broth.

15. In a large pot, heat up remaining tbsp of oil over a medium heat.

16. Add mushrooms and brown until tender.

17. Pour in broth and season to taste with soy sauce.

18. Reduce to a simmer and then reduce the heat again to low.

19. Partially cover pot and simmer until warm.

20. Whisk in miso.

21. In the meantime, cook the ramen noodles in a pot of boiling water for 2–3 minutes.

22. When cooked, divide noodles between bowls and ladle broth over the ramen.

23. Top with sweet potato and garnish with green onions.

24. Enjoy piping hot!

Vegan Ramen with Kimchi

Kimchi and ramen is too good a combination to not include a second time but in a veggie version!

 2 bowls

 15 mins

Ingredients:

- 3 cups water
- 1/2 cup well-fermented kimchi
- 1/4 cup bean sprouts
- 1 tbsp white rice wine
- 1 tsp extra light olive oil
- 1 tsp sesame oil
- 1 tsp rice vinegar
- 1 tsp smoked paprika
- 1 tsp low-sodium soy sauce
- 1/2 tsp red chili flakes

- 1/4 tsp salt

- A few sprinkles of Szechuan peppercorns

- 2 pkts Japanese ramen noodles

- 1 scallion

- 1–2 tablespoons well-fermented kimchi

Instructions:

1. In a medium-sized pot pour in the 3 cups of water then add the bean sprouts, kimchi, olive oil, sesame oil, rice vinegar, red chili flakes, salt, peppercorns, paprika, soy sauce and ramen.

2. Stir everything well together and bring heat up to the boil.

3. Cook for 5–10 minutes, or until the ramen is cooked through.

4. Slice the scallions into thin strips.

5. Once ramen is cooked, ladle the whole mixture of ramen and soup into the bowls and garnish with the scallions and kimchi.

6. Enjoy!

Vegan Kale and Shiitake Mushroom Winter Ramen

This tasty ramen packed full of mushrooms is hearty and substantial and perfect to slurp up to keep you going on a winter day!

 2 bowls

 30 mins

Ingredients:

- 2 tbsps olive oil

- 2 green onions, sliced

- 1 cup loosely packed sliced flat leafed kale

- 1/2 cup sliced shiitake mushrooms

- 3/4 tsp ginger powder

- 1/2 tsp kosher salt

- 1/4 tsp black pepper

- 1 tsp chili garlic sauce

- 2–3 cups vegetable stock

- 2 pkts Japanese ramen noodles

- Sriracha drizzling on top

Instructions:

1. In a skillet, heat oil over a medium-high heat.

2. Add mushrooms, kale and green onions when oil is hot.

3. Fry the vegetables until they just begin to get soft.

4. Add salt, pepper, ginger and chili garlic sauce.

5. Stir together and pour in vegetable stock.

6. Turn up heat to allow soup to boil and then add ramen noodles and cook for 2–3 minutes.

7. Remove soup from heat and divide into two bowls.

8. Drizzle with sriracha for a good kick and serve!

Vegan Tofu and Shiitake Mushroom Ramen Bowl

You're making your own broth for this delicious and filling mushroom and tofu ramen bowl! The Kombu seaweed gives it an additional wonderful layer of flavor.

 2 bowls

 1 hour 45 mins

Ingredients:

- 1 onion, chopped

- 1 tbsp oil

- 6 cups water

- 1 cup (1 oz) dried shiitake mushrooms

- 1 sheet kombu seaweed (available at Asian markets)

- 5 crushed cloves garlic

- Ground pepper

- 1/4 cup mirin

- 1/4 cup soy sauce, more to taste

- 2 pkts Japanese ramen noodles

- 8 ozs cubed tofu

- 1 cup chopped scallions

- toasted sesame oil

- Sriracha sauce

- 4 ozs fresh shiitake mushrooms, de-stemmed and sliced.

Instructions:

1. In a large pot over medium-high heat fry the onion in oil until tender, for about 3 minutes.

2. Turn down heat to medium and cook onions until golden brown.

3. Pour in water and soy sauce, mirin, pepper, garlic, kombu seaweed and 1 cup of mushrooms.

4. Bring to a boil.

5. Lower heat and simmer for 30 minutes uncovered on a medium heat and then remove seaweed.

6. Simmer pot for a further 15–20 minutes and then strain.

7. Taste for salt content. You should end up with 6–8 cups of broth. Add water if it is too salty.

8. Simmer another 15–20 minutes. Strain. Keep warm. This will reduce and you will end up with 6–8 cups. Taste for salt. If this reduces by more than half, it may become too salty... so add a little water to taste.

9. Heat a skillet and add a little oil and toss in other shiitake mushrooms. Cook until moisture is released and they brown.

10. Cook ramen noodles in a pot of boiling water for 2–3 minutes and then drain.

11. Divide noodles between two bowls and pour over broth. Fill with the mushrooms and tofu and drizzle over sesame oil and sriracha.

12. Garnish with scallions and cilantro and serve hot!

Vegan Thai Green Curry Ramen

This delicious Thai green curry is a wonderful way to use ramen noodles and will impress your friends **and family!**

 2 bowls

 20 mins

Ingredients:

- 2 tbsps coconut oil or peanut oil

- Green curry paste

- 4 small green Thai chilis

- 1/2 cup shallot, chopped

- 4 cloves garlic, chopped

- 2 thumb-sized pieces ginger

- 1 stalk lemongrass

- 1/2 tsp ground white pepper

- 2 tbsps fish sauce

- 3 tsps brown sugar

- 2 tbsps lime juice

- Salt

- 1 small onion, large diced

- 2 cups carrots, large diced

- 2 cups oyster mushroom, large diced

- 1/2 can coconut milk

- 1/2 can water

- 2 kaffir lime leaves (or, as substitute, 1 tsp grated lime zest)

- 2 pkts Japanese ramen noodles

- 1 cup bean sprouts, washed

- 2 radishes, washed and thinly sliced

- 1/2 cup red onion, thinly sliced

- Handful fresh Thai basil and cilantro, washed and dried

Instructions:

1. Heat up olive oil in a large pot over a medium-high heat.

2. Add curry paste, shallots, garlic, ginger, chilis, lemongrass and onion.

3. Fry for about 2–3 minutes and add coconut milk and water.

4. Bring heat up to let curry boil and then reduce to a simmer.

5. Add carrots and cover pot.

6. Simmer for 5 minutes whilst stirring occasionally.

7. In the meantime, fill another pot of water and bring to boil.

8. Place ramen noodles in water and cook for 2–3 minutes and drain.

9. Put oyster mushrooms, lime leaves and zest, pepper and brown sugar in curry and mix well.

10. Simmer for 5–10 minutes and then add fish sauce and lime juice.

11. Season to personal preference and adjust flavors if you wish. If is too spicy then add more coconut milk.

12. Mix cooked ramen into curry and turn off heat.

13. Stir well and then divide into two bowls.

14. Garnish with herbs, bean sprouts and radish and serve.

Spiced and Garlicky Ramen Soup

This tasty spiced vegetarian soup is wonderfully fragrant and bolstering!

 2 bowls

 20 mins

Ingredients:

- 1 cup coconut milk

- 2/3 cup chopped tomatoes, no salt added

- 2 large cloves garlic, roughly chopped

- 1-inch piece fresh ginger, peeled and rough chopped

- 1 and 1/2 tsp wheat-free tamari

- 1 tsp agave syrup

- 2 tsps fish sauce

- 2 tsps toasted sesame oil

- 1 tsp chili powder

- 1/2 tsp ground cinnamon

- 1/2 tsp ground coriander

- 1/2 tsp curry powder

- 1/2 tsp ground fennel

- 1/4 tsp ground cumin

- 3 cups vegetable stock

- 2 carrots, thinly sliced on the diagonal

- 1 cup broccoli florets

- 2 pkts Japanese ramen noodles

- 2 boiled eggs

- sliced scallions, cilantro, jalapeño, lime and sriracha, for scrving (optional)

Instructions:

1. Pour the first 14 ingredients (coconut milk to cumin) in a blender or food processor and blend until tomatoes, ginger and garlic are in puree form.

2. Pour in vegetable stock and blend again.

3. Pour mix into a large pot and bring to boil.

4. Reduce heat and simmer for about 10 minutes.

5. Add carrots and broccoli and cook for about 1–2 minutes or until tender.

6. In the meantime, fill a pot with water and bring to the boil for ramen noodles.

7. Add ramen to pot and cook for 2–3 minutes.

8. Divide noodles between bowls and ladle over soup.

9. Top with veggies and garnish with scallions, cilantro, jalapeños, sriracha and boiled eggs.

10. Enjoy hot!

Vegan Ramen Butternut Squash Bowl

The combination of butternut squash and Sambal Oelek make for a tasty dish elevated to new heights with toasty sesame oil and seeds.

 2 bowls

 15 mins

Ingredients:

- 2 cups veggie stock
- 3 cups butternut squash
- 1/2 tsp salt
- 1/2 tsp soy sauce
- 2 pkts Japanese ramen noodles
- 1/2 cup medium soft tofu, rinsed and cubed
- 2 scallions, sliced
- 1/2 tsp Sambal Oelek chili paste

- 1 tsp toasted sesame oil

- Handful fresh spinach

- Black sesame seeds

Instructiions:

1. Begin by putting the butternut squash in a blender or food processor and blending until it is pureed.

2. Combine the pureed butternut squash and broth in a medium pot and stir together.

3. Season with salt and soy sauce and heat up for about 3–4 minutes until mixture is lightly boiling.

4. As the mixture is heating up, cut the tofu up into small pieces.

5. Slice green onion and wash spinach.

6. Heat up a pot of boiling water and add ramen noodles and cook for 2–3 minutes.

7. Divide noodles into bowls and pour broth over each bowl.

8. Sprinkle over piece of tofu into each bowl and put in a little Sambal Oelek.

9. Pour sesame oil into bowls along with sesame seeds to garnish.

10. Serve and enjoy!

WEIRD & WONDERFUL RAMEN

Authentic ramen is wonderful, we know that. But this is the 21st century and there are wilder ways of cooking this wonderful foodstuff than ever before—including sweet dishes! In this bonus chapter I've included my favorite 'weird and wonderful' ramen dishes!

Rapid Ramen Burger

You're probably familiar with this popular trend by now! The ramen burger has been taking the foodie world by storm for a while now, so why not try your hand at making one of your own? The below amounts make one burger, so simply double up for more!

 1 portion

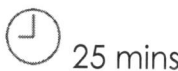 25 mins

Ingredients:

- 1 pkt Japanese ramen noodles

- 2 eggs, divided into yolk and white

- 2 tbsps canola oil

- 1 tbsp ketchup

- 1/2 tbsp sriracha

- 1 beef burger patty

- Soy sauce

- Sesame oil

- 1 slice Cheddar Cheese

- 1 scallion, thinly sliced

Instructions:

1. Fill a pot with boiling water, add ramen and cook for 2–3 minutes and then drain.

2. Let cool to room temperature.

3. In a small bowl, whisk 1 egg well and mix in the ramen and coat thoroughly with egg.

4. Divide the egg-soaked ramen into 2 portions and place each portion into a ramekin or similar small bowl.

5. Cover ramen with Clingfilm and place can of soup or equivalent over each portion of ramen in the bowls in order to squish them into a bun shape.

6. Put in refrigerator for 15 minutes at least.

7. Add oil to skillet and heat over medium-high heat.

8. When oil is hot, place the shaped ramen buns in pan and flip and fry until a golden brown on both sides.

9. In a separate bowl whisk together sriracha and ketchup.

10. Season your burger patty with the salt, pepper, soy sauce and sesame oil and add any extras you might like.

11. Wipe skillet and fry burger over medium-high heat to your preference. I personally like medium rare.

12. Place burger aside on plate and top with a slice of cheese and drizzle of sesame oil.

13. Lower skillet's heat to medium and add a little extra oil and fry an egg sunny side up.

14. On a plate you assemble your tasty ramen burger as so: ramen bun, ketchup, burger (with melted cheese on top), fried egg, sliced scallions and top with second ramen bun.

15. Get that beautiful thing in two hands and dig in whilst it's hot!

Ramen Pizza

The first of our unorthodox ramen delights! Share this unique pie with friends and family. It's guaranteed to go down a storm, and feel free to substitute toppings.

 6 portions

 20 mins

Ingredients:

- 8 cups water

- 4 pkts Japanese ramen noodles

- 1 tbsp olive oil

- 1 can spaghetti sauce or equivalent

- 4 ozs mozzarella or any grated cheese

- 17 slices pepperoni

- 1/2 tsp dried oregano

Instructions:

1. Add water to a large pot and boil. Add ramen noodles and cook for 2–3 minutes or until done and drain.

2. Heat olive oil in a large oven-proof skillet over a medium heat.

3. When the oil is hot, add the cooked ramen and press down evenly so that the bottom of the pan is covered.

4. Cook for 2 minutes or until golden and brown underneath.

5. Spread sauce over noodles and then sprinkle with grated cheese, pepperoni and oregano.

6. Place skillet in oven for approx. 3–5 minutes or until cheese is starting to bubble and brown.

7. Leave to cool for about 5 minutes before cutting up and serving!

Ricotta Ramen Frittata

I was skeptical at first about this unusual frittata but it works a dream—a great addition for a buffet table!

 6 portions

 35 mins

Ingredients:

- 2 cups frozen green peas
- 3 pkts Japanese ramen noodles
- 1 container ricotta cheese
- 1 tbsp soy sauce
- 3 large eggs
- 1/2 cup milk
- 1/2 cup grated Parmesan cheese
- 1/4 tsp pepper
- 1 can tomatoes

Instructions:

1. Heat up oven to 400°F.

2. Lightly grease a 13 x 9-inch baking pan or dish.

3. Fill a large pot with water, add frozen peas and turn up heat to boil.

4. Add noodles to boiling water and cook for 2–3 minutes or until noodles and peas are cooked and drain.

5. In the meantime, mix ricotta, eggs, milk, Parmesan, pepper and soy sauce in a bowl until incorporated.

6. Mix in cooked noodles and peas.

7. Pour mixture into a prepared baking dish and spread evenly out.

8. Bake for about 20 minutes or until set and remove.

9. Heat the tomatoes gently in a saucepan until hot and slightly reduced. Season with salt and pepper if you like.

10. Pour tomatoes over frittata and cut into nice big chunks to serve.

Grilled Cheese and Bacon Ramen

A twist on the American classic! Bolstering carbs packed full of cheddar cheese and juicy bacon. What's not to love?

 1 portion

30 mins

Ingredients:

- 2 pkts Japanese ramen noodles

- 1/2 tbsp olive oil

- 2 large eggs

- 1 cup grated cheddar cheese

- 6 slices bacon

- Sprig fresh parsley for garnish

Instructions:

1. Bring water to boil in a pot and cook ramen for 2–3 minutes. Remove from heat before fully cooked and too soft.

2. Drain and rinse ramen under cold water and put aside in a bowl and allow to cool down.

3. Crack and beat the eggs in with the noodles, using a spoon.

4. Place the noodles on a chopping board and shape them into two large rectangles about 1/2 inch thick.

5. Cut the rectangles in half to form 2 squares.

6. Place the 4 square slices on parchment or wax paper and wrap up the slices in the paper.

7. Refrigerate for 20 minutes.

8. Heat the oil in a skillet over medium heat.

9. Place 1 ramen slice in the skillet. Fry for 2 to 3 minutes or until lightly browned and golden and flip to the other side and repeat frying time until both sides are golden brown.

10. Remove slice and repeat previous step for other slices of ramen.

11. As soon as the second slice of ramen is flipped for each grilled cheese, top with the grated cheese so that it can melt on top.

12. In another skillet or under the grill, cook the bacon for 3–4 minutes.

13. Lay bacon strips on top of the cheesy ramen slices.

14. Top the cheese and bacon ramen with the other slice of ramen and remove from heat.

15. Garnish with a sprig of parsley and enjoy hot!

Crunchy and Spicy Ramen Trail Mix

Sick of your boring old trail mix? Who knew that packet ramen could be so versatile? Instant ramen added with plenty of other tasty treats is easily portable and a great snack to have on the go. It's best to make a decently sized batch of this to keep for when you have a snack hankering!

 18 portions

 20 mins

Ingredients:

- 2 pkts Japanese ramen noodles broken into small pieces

- 1 cup raw cashews

- 1 cup raw peanuts

- 1 cup cornflakes

- 3 tbsps vegetable oil

- 4 tsps curry powder

- 1/2 tsp cayenne pepper

- 1/2 tsp fine salt

- 1/2 cup freeze-dried wasabi peas

Instructions:

1. Preheat oven to 750°F.

2. Line a baking sheet.

3. In a bowl mix ramen, cashews, peanuts, and cornflakes with oil until all pieces are coated.

4. Spread out mixture in an even layer over baking sheet.

5. In another bowl mix curry powder, cayenne and salt in a separate small bowl.

6. Pour over ramen mixture.

7. Bake in oven for about 10 minutes or until golden brown and make sure to stir 2 times whilst cooking.

8. Take out of oven and mix in wasabi peas.

9. Lave to cool completely before eating!

Peanut Butter and Chocolate Ramen Fridge Bars

Would you have thought that ramen would be a good ingredient in a sweet treat? Just try your hand at these tasty chocolate and peanut bars and you'll see why it's a great fit!

 8 portions

2 hours 15 minutes (2 hours for bars to set)

Ingredients:

- Cooking spray

- 1 pkt Japanese ramen noodles, crushed

- 1 can (10 ozs) sweetened condensed milk

- 1/4 tsp salt

- 1/2 cup powdered sugar

- 1/2 cup smooth peanut butter

- 1 cup milk chocolate chips

Instructions:

1. Place parchment paper in a baking pan and spray with cooking spray.

2. Place crushed ramen, condensed milk, salt, powdered sugar and peanut butter in a bowl and mix thoroughly together.

3. Pour mixture into baking pan and spread out evenly.

4. Microwave chocolate chips on a medium setting for around 45 seconds. Stir and microwave for 15 seconds more or until melted. If you don't have a microwave then melt the chocolate over a small boiling pan of water in a heatproof bowl and stir until melted.

5. Pour melted chocolate over the ramen mixture in the pan until completely covered.

6. Place in fridge for 2 hours until set.

7. Cut into chunky squares and enjoy!

23956088R00085

Printed in Poland
by Amazon Fulfillment
Poland Sp. z o.o., Wrocław